10 IDEAS TO SAVE 10% IN 10 MINUTES

MONEY, TIME AND EFFICIENCY IDEAS FOR THE MODERN PROFESSIONAL

JUSTIN TURNER

A CIP catalogue record of this book is available from the British Library.

ISBN (Paperback): 978-1-7396720-2-7

ISBN (ebook): 978-1-7396720-3-4

Imprint: AskJT LTD

Edited by: Steven Holmberg

For further information about this book, please contact the author at: www.askjt.co.uk

For Benji, James and Sue

INTRODUCTION

So can you read this book in 10 minutes? No, but the idea is that you can read each chapter in 10 minutes or less. Plus, it will spark ideas and lead you on a path to save at least 10% in all sorts of places.

The book is a quick read and is designed as a pocket guide. I've developed ideas most people won't think about when searching for ways to save time and money. In order to keep the book engaging and easy to read, I'll not be going into any in-depth analysis or minute details. You may need to do some research after I've given you the starting point.

In a world ravaged by inflation and soaring costs, we could all do with some extra help. I had my accountancy clients in mind when I started writing. My clients often say things like "Why wasn't I taught this stuff at school?" so it seems apt to develop a resource to provide inspiration.

Most of the ideas cost nothing to implement, but a few of them need some investment, so they might not be for everyone. I haven't been paid to endorse any product or service. If

I mention a product, I only do so based on my experience using it.

This book isn't just about financial savings. It also embraces the broader quest for saving time. Time is a precious commodity in our lives, so this book is crafted to unlock additional hours for you, hopefully paving the way to a life rich with fulfilment, joy, and adventure.

Some of the ideas contained within revolve around technology; some are old-fashioned principles and ideas reworked for the modern world.

If you enjoy this book, consider my longer book "The Science of Business." You can also find other useful materials on my @Ask_JT YouTube channel or by visiting askjt.co.uk.

1

THE SECRET KEY

One day my wife was at work and couldn't find her keys to the house. She checked her car. She checked her pockets. She even rummaged into the deep dark depths of her handbag! But to no avail. I found her keys later that day when I returned home. They were hanging on the outside of the door, in full view of the passing public! Anyone could have just unlocked the house and helped themselves to our property. But in the context of this book, here's what is most noteworthy: *she and I both wasted time looking for the keys.*

In the hustle of our daily lives, we all overlook small inefficiencies that chip away at our time. Research suggests that the average person spends 2.5 days each year looking for lost things, with keys ranking high among frequently misplaced items.

. . .

When my eldest son started secondary school, we realised that he would need a key to the house. However, as anyone with children of this age knows, these miniature marvels are teeming with delightful flaws. One such flaw is the uncanny knack of misplacing essential items. Just how many times would my son lose his house key?!

I didn't want to wait to discover the answer to that question. So I tried to envision a world where my son could effortlessly enter his home without needing a key. Perhaps with a simple code, fingerprint, or tap on his smartphone.

Enter the era of the smart lock. It's a technological marvel that promises to not only secure our homes but also to streamline our routines. A smart lock allows keyless entry, grants temporary access to visitors, and gives children access without the risk of lost keys. Smart locks represent a significant leap towards convenience and efficiency.

They turn the stress of misplaced keys and frantic searches into things of the past. You might be thinking this isn't such a big issue but stress is a big issue. All these small things like losing your keys add to the stress of life. They cost you valuable time that you can't afford to waste. And that wasted time creates even more stress as you try to catch up.

"Dad, where is my rugby kit?" "Dad, where are my running shoes?" "Mum, where have you put my football boots?" "Have you seen my laptop?"

. . .

Why wouldn't we want to get rid of at least one question – "Have you seen my keys?"

Smart locks provide other advantages. Letting a tradesperson, delivery driver, or neighbour into the house without anyone having to be home is tremendously helpful. I once went away for the night and forgot to feed my two hungry cats. I simply messaged a friend and sent them an access code to the house. This is all time saved and more importantly it saves stress and worry.

It's not just the time it takes to find your keys but the time it takes to unlock the door. Picture the situation where you're carrying shopping bags whilst rooting around in your pocket or handbag for the key. With a smart lock, I simply press my finger against the scanner at my door, and I'm in. I save several seconds, and that really adds up over time. I can drop off my children at home before I nip down to the local shop and I don't need to worry about mum needing to come to the door to let them in. They can just use their own fingerprint to gain access.

Our house has also become more secure. In the past, we had a traditional mortice lock, so unless someone physically turned the key, the house was left open. My wife used to wake up in the middle of the night worrying if we'd locked the front door. So there is a great saving in stress not worrying about if you and the family are secure.

. . .

It's wonderful how the smart lock is as close to frictionless as possible. As soon as you close the door it is locked. When you leave the house just pull down the handle and the door unlocks automatically (no internal locking mechanism). It doesn't matter if the door locks behind you as it's a simple fingerprint to get back in. I know several people who have locked themselves out of their house when they have standard deadlocks. We've just removed even more worries!

I think adopting smart locks also aligns with broader trends in home automation and smart home technology. $4.4 billion is the projected value of the smart lock market by 2027. You see, an expanding market like this tends to only expand because products solve a real problem and are easy for the consumer to understand. In other words, just don't take it from me about the effectiveness of smart locks. Broader trends are proving that everyone else is waking up to this new technology.

Will it save 10%? If you factor in time, stress and convenience, it gets my vote.

Top Tips:

- Choose a smart lock with a fingerprint scanner. This is the easiest and fastest way to get into your home. I have 7 options to access my home and I find the fingerprint is always fastest.

- Choose a good quality product. The lock is an investment in the future so do some research. I installed the Simpled Smart Lock, which is excellent for battery life and usability.
- As with many technology devices, they require batteries, so invest in good quality, high-capacity rechargeable batteries. They'll save you a fortune, not only with your smart lock but also with other items around your home.
- Integrating technology such as AirTags with everyday items further mitigates the problem of lost possessions.

2

TURN UP THE HEAT

When we were looking for our forever home my wife found a house on one of the property portals. "I'm not moving to the village of the damned!" I said, when I saw the location of the property. The area didn't exactly have the best reputation. "Let's just go and take a look," my wife suggested.

Oh dear! Bad mistake. When I walked through the front door for the first viewing I knew I'd already bought the house. I'd fallen in love. Several months later we had the keys.

Our house is a stone built, converted farm house constructed in the 1800s. For our living room we've got what's called a Gin Gang, the circular structure where a horse walked round and round to make flour. This all sounds perfect, doesn't it? For the most part it is, except there's a horrifying secret.

. . .

You see, building regulations and insulation were not hot topics back in the 1800s. The big secret is how much my gas bill is! I'll not tell you the amount but it's more than I pay for my mortgage. I dread the winter months as my heating costs become almost unbearable. There is no scope for traditional insulation solutions like cavity wall or loft insulation. These would, of course, be the first place to start.

So a few years ago I went on a journey to do something about heating costs. I'd already forked out for solar panels and a battery so my electricity usage was under control, but the gas usage was still a significant problem. I only had a small budget so there was no scope for something like a heat pump.

So how did I solve the issue? Let me introduce you to smart heating controls. These devices are designed to learn from your habits and then automatically adjust your home's temperature. It's a fusion of convenience and efficiency. There are two main types of controls: those that replace your main home's thermostat and others to replace thermostatic radiator valves.

In the realm of household energy consumption, a staggering 80% is attributed to heating and hot water. For those of you familiar with Pareto's 80/20 principle, this won't surprise you. Check out my first book "The Science of Business" where I discuss how you can use Pareto's principle in greater detail.

To solve my own usage problem, I found a company called Tado, a manufacturer of smart heating controls. Tado was making an ambitious claim of a 31% reduction in heating bills. I decided to give Tado a try and, to make a long story short, I saw a more modest yet still significant savings of 17% in my heating costs. This indeed proved a testament to the potential of smart heating controls.

But why am I suggesting them here? When I first came across the heating controls, the price of purchasing and installing them put me off. But these controls offered full recovery on the initial cost in just over a year, and that's a quick return on investment. (In contrast, a photovoltaic system I installed has a 7-9 year return on the initial investment.) According to my own data, the smart heating controls clearly added up to a 10% or more saving.

Realising that my costly heating and water heating were the chief culprits in my energy expenditure led me to seek innovative solutions. The installation of smart thermostats and radiator valves marked the beginning of a new chapter in my home's energy story. Through their precise control and adaptability, these intelligent systems have not only enhanced the comfort of my living spaces but also carved a significant chunk out of my energy bills.

.   .   .

The evidence supporting the efficacy of smart heating controls is robust. For instance, a study by the UK Government revealed that while traditional heating controls offer marginal savings, the advent of smart controls has the potential to revolutionise household energy consumption patterns. Similarly, American research highlights the dramatic cost-effectiveness of smart heating systems, with return on investment periods astonishingly short compared to other green technologies.

The adoption of smart heating controls in my own home supported these findings. My initial scepticism was quickly dispelled when I witnessed a marked reduction in energy usage and the subsequent, tangible savings on my bills. The system's ability to maintain optimal temperatures without constant human intervention is nothing short of revolutionary.

Beyond the benefits to my own life, smart heating controls embody even broader principles of sustainability and environmental stewardship. By optimising energy use, these systems play a crucial role in reducing households' carbon footprint, aligning with global efforts to combat climate change.

The story of smart heating controls is not just about the warmth they provide or the savings they offer. It is about a narrative of innovation, environmental responsibility, and data-driven decisions that continues to evolve as more households embrace the future of home heating.

.   .   .

I have a free e-learning course called "Going Eco" on my askjt.co.uk website. In it, I look at my home's photovoltaic power system, smart energy tariffs, and smart heating controls.

Top tips:

- I bought some of my controls on Black Friday deals and some as refurbished items, both of which gave me good savings of over 10% compared to the recommended retail price.
- The end of summer is the best time to install the controls and the perfect time to test your heating system. Lots of boiler breakdowns happen when we first turn on the heating so why not test them nice and early?
- Find a product which is easy to install yourself. Tado's app had easy step by step instructions to follow so I installed all the controls myself. The thermostatic valves were easy to install with no particular skills needed, but the wall mounted controls did need connection to the power system. So if you're not comfortable with electrical work, hire a qualified electrician.

I've mentioned Tado as just one example. There are many other providers on the market. Do some research because what was right for me might not be the perfect solution for you.

3

BEAT THE BANK

B efore I start this chapter I need to give out some advice, so please take note. I talk about the use of credit cards. Please <u>be careful</u> whenever you are using or taking out a credit card. When you can't pay the balance in full, the banks are going to win...and I want you to win. Set up a direct debit to pay the balance in full each month and keep your spending to the essentials. Just because you have credit doesn't mean you have an excuse to make extravagant purchases. I've seen the stats on UK credit card debt per household and it's not easy reading. If you do already have credit card debts that you'd like to clear, then Chapter 7 is going to help. There is also some useful information at the end of this particular chapter about non credit card strategies, so do read it in full.

Now, a brief story...

. . .

It wasn't too long until my youngest son's birthday, and he requested a Lego set. A quick search told me the set would cost £50. But what could I do to reduce that cost?

If you're like me, you'll usually search around for the best price. A quick search told me that I could buy the Lego set from a large department store at the same price as the Lego store. However, if I bought it from the department store, I would be able to get an additional 3% cash back on the purchase. Easy decision to make! I'll explain how it all worked a bit later in this chapter.

This story is an example of how there are strategies brimming with potential within all transactions. This chapter will educate you about how to maximise all this potential by showing you various strategies to gain savings... savings that can add up to that all-important 10% when you put them all together.

The first place to start is to find a credit card or charge card offering a cashback of 1% on all purchases. Simple as that. 1% back on things like your daily shop.

What's the next place to save some money?

Many large organisations around the world offer something called affiliate marketing, or what we can simply call referral marketing. This is a system where an organisation pays you a commission if you refer a customer to their website and that customer makes a purchase.

Using referral marketing can be done in various ways, a common one being websites that specialise in cashback. Sure, these websites want to make money for themselves, but they are very willing to share some of the spoils with you. For example, that 3% saving on my son's Lego set was part of a referral scheme setup by my credit card company. It worked by finding a promotion in the app where I manage my credit card. You click on the promotion, which takes you to the retailer's website. Shortly after you check-out, the cash back lands in your account. The credit card companies use a special tracking mechanism so the retailer can pay the credit card company the commission.

The company makes it easy to find but you do need to check the promotions section prior to buying. So get in the habit of checking for offers before buying. And remember, the 3% Lego savings was on top of the 1% cashback I was already getting by simply using the cashback credit card for the Lego purchase.

Another example is when I purchased my last dishwasher. I gained a cashback of 6%! I found an appliance retailer on a cashback website and just clicked the link. I did need to set up an account with the cashback website, but a few minutes later my cashback was showing in my account. Using a cash-back website is a great way to earn cash on essential purchases such as insurance.

. . .

There are loads of referral opportunities on cashback websites. Just Google "cashback website," and you'll get loads of referral websites to choose from. Each website lays out ways for you to refer people and gain commissions.

Of course, referrals can also involve friends and family. Who do you know that might take advantage of a good product or company...and let you make a few extra referral pounds for yourself? If you know of a great product or service, make a suggestion to a friend or family member. Keep in mind it's always a good idea to ask if they're keen to be referred.

For example, I could refer myself when I purchased my electric car in order to gain £250 cash back. I was going to buy a replacement electric vehicle from the same company, but this time, I bought it through my business. The car company had a dedicated area on its website called Promotions. The instructions were there to follow, so I clicked on the link, which took me to the purchase page, and £250 came off the list price. I used the same principle with my utility company. Every time I log into my utility account online, a link says "refer a friend, and we'll pay each of you £50." I sent my mum the link when she was looking to switch utility providers. We each had £50 taken off our utility bill a couple of weeks later. I've shared this link with several family members so everyone can benefit from the £50. But it's not just utility companies – many of your usual household favourites will have referral links.

. . .

All the strategies I've laid out so far are not about gaming the system but rather about seizing opportunities made available by large corporations. The strengths of these strategies lie in their simplicity and accessibility. They don't require a high degree of skill or insider knowledge, just a willingness to engage with the tools and opportunities available to every consumer.

Ok, we've discovered many ways to get our way closer to an overall 10% saving. How do we actually get all the way there?

Another great idea is to take advantage of retailers' loyalty schemes. For example, the supermarket that I regularly use for my food shop offers a 1% cashback on all purchases. How it works is that I get back 1% of my total food purchases in points. I can then choose to exchange these points for a cash deduction on my current purchase, or I can accumulate the points over time.

A further advantage is gained if I choose the option to turn my credit card cash back into discounted gift cards. How this works is I choose a gift card for the same supermarket I'm already shopping in. The points allow me to get a 2% discount on the amount of the card. For example, if I use my points to get a £100 gift card, the card only costs me £98. And when I later use that gift card, I continue to still get the 1% worth of loyalty points! I admit that the points earned when using the gift card aren't massive, but it all adds up.

· · ·

An even further bonus comes when I can double my accumulated supermarket loyalty points to pay for a Channel Tunnel during a family campervan holiday. The supermarket has an online login to a membership area where you can see available referral partners. This allows you to see opportunities to double the points when you spend with the referral partner. It's just a case of clicking the link.

The cost of my last channel crossing was £150 but I had £50 of loyalty points. So I doubled these to £100 worth of points just by finding the referral partner on the website login. So I'm now only paying £50 for what should be a £150 crossing. I don't want to mislead you by saying this is a 100% saving, as I still had something left to pay. But I did save 100% of the £100 I would have otherwise spent.

Going on holiday is a luxury but, just like you, when I go on holiday I want savings. I'm lucky the tunnel crossing is one of the available retailers and meets the requirements of our holiday plans. Plus our holiday is already part of our annual household expenditure. In other words, I'm not spending money on something I wouldn't normally spend money on, simply to get a discount on it.

Finding a partner that suits your needs on a loyalty scheme is not always possible. And it's not always something you have an "essential" need to spend money on. Here is a fun idea, why don't you pick your holiday based on available deals? You never know, you might find your new preferred holiday destination.

Let's finish up – how are we on our path to 10% overall savings? 1% cash back, 1% on loyalty points, 2% discount on my gift card and 100% on the channel crossing. So are the savings actually over 104%?

In the past, I employed this strategy of combining various savings but never really thought about totting up the numbers. It's hard to express the total savings as a single percentage because the calculations reflect varying bases. I understand that we can't really just add all these percentages together to reach a final, all-encompassing savings.

But let's put that complexity to one side and suffice it to say that we've achieved our goal of maximising our savings as best we can.

Top tips:

- Even when referrals aren't available, it's sometimes possible to buy a discounted gift card from the retailer you're going to shop at. Then just do your shopping with the gift card knowing you've purchased it at a discount.
- If you own a business, you might find that a cash back card is going to result in a huge saving.

Especially if you find one that allows you to turn the points into gift cards. Did you know that your business can give you a gift card of £50 as a gift? No tax is due on the gift. In fact you can have up to £300 worth of gift cards from your own business each year without tax being due. As long as the gift cards are £50 or under each. This is an example of a little loophole called trivial benefits. But do speak to a tax professional before doing things like this as certain conditions need to be met.

- Cashback websites do collect data from you. So be careful about what you share and the email address you use. I use a separate email for my online shopping to give me extra protection. Plus there are plenty of scams around so do your research before you buy.

4

COOKING UP A STORM

I'm going to take you on a gastronomic journey where the resulting dish is a few extra pennies.

"I only married him for his cooking," my wife announces!

My wife Sue made that statement when visiting a regular client to do their weekly bookkeeping. While the client might be thrilled with the work, there is an envy amongst the staff about something else that gained real attention – the contents of the lunchbox. The staff drooled with envy as she opened the box to reveal what was inside. It's usually the leftovers from something I've cooked or maybe a nice salad. (Stop thinking about the lettuce – there is more to salad than Iceberg.) On this particular occasion, lunch was homemade bread, an avocado, tomato, and basil salad, and home-cooked chicken. And let's not forget the balsamic drizzle rounding off this open sandwich. You see, she really did marry me just for my cooking!

·　·　·

My journey as a cook all started when I was 16, and my mum (a single parent) declared that I needed to provide some meals. Over the course of one summer holiday, I began to learn to cook. I'm still learning, and I'm learning about techniques and flavours from different cultures. I've visited the world from within my kitchen I've travelled the world, and nothing is too far out of my skills. My humble point here is: I've become an excellent cook.

Why is this important? Well, I don't need fancy statistics to tell you that a takeaway is far more expensive than cooking for yourself.

Plus, when I get takeaway food I'm often disappointed. It takes ages to come, it's cold, it doesn't taste as good as I hoped, and my bank account took a hit. What should be a convenience turns out not to be. Why didn't I just make it myself?

Why a chapter about this in the book? Food accounts for 11.76% of a UK household's weekly expenditure, with takeaway and restaurant eating the most expensive. That represents something like 15% on our food essentials and eating out. I found another statistic indicating that in the UK an average household will spend over £1,200 per annum in restaurants and on takeaways. So if we're looking to save some money, food is a major part of the journey. The average earner in the UK makes just under £28,000 per annum. So most of us will be spending around £4,200 on food each year. Can we save 10% on that amount? Can we save £420?

In the UK in 2022, we spent £1.91 billion on chilled ready meals. That's about £28 for every person in the UK. If you only count the adults then that amount quickly jumps up. It gets even higher when you consider that not everyone is buying ready meals. I think for a large number of people – the ones actually accounting for ready meal spending – we can definitely save money on our food!

In an era where convenience food reigns supreme, the cost of pre-packaged meals or dining out has become a significant portion of household expenditure.

Here are a few quick tips to save on your food bills:

Learn to cook

The biggest saving you can make on the food front is to learn to cook. The sooner you drop ready meals in favour of your wok, oven, or frying pan, the sooner the savings will start.

Plan the week

I saw a terrifying article a few years ago which said a third of all food is wasted. A significant portion of this waste happens due to people throwing away food because of poor planning. If you plan your meals in advance, you'll buy less, have less food waste, and keep more money in your pocket.

Use your freezer

The freezer is the best way of preserving food so put it in before it's too late. Have a monthly audit of what's in your freezer and eat what's in there before you buy anymore. You'll be amazed by the number of things you can freeze. Just ask Google what can be frozen!

Kitchen Gadgets

Potato ricer, egg slicer, a raft of knives, cake tins, and a proving basket are all things you can find in my kitchen. I've got all the plug-in stuff as well, from juicers to mixers. But there is one gadget that has blown me away. It is my Ninja Foodi multi-cooker. It's a pressure cooker, dehydrator, mini roasting oven, air fryer, steamer, grill, slow cooker, yoghurt maker, and frying pan all rolled into one. I understand buying gadgets can be daunting because they are costly and you have to learn how to use them. But the multi cooker eliminates the need for separate appliances. An appliance like this tends to use less energy to run than a conventional oven, so it's brilliant for couples and people living on their own who want to avoid turning on the main oven. However, don't get carried away with gadgets. They can promise to save you time and money but often end up at the back of a cupboard. It's better to invest in quality products like my multi cooker because it gives you many different methods of cooking.

· · ·

Crisps vs popcorn

I buy 2kg bags of popcorn kernels for just over £6. That makes a huge amount of popcorn. In contrast, my local supermarket sells pre-popped salted popcorn at £1.41 per a paltry 100g. Popcorn is super easy to make in a large pan in about 2 minutes. So why not pop some for a movie instead of other snacks? Or bag up some spare popcorn for mid morning snacks and children's lunches. It's both healthier and much less expensive.

Preserving

I love pickled, sliced red onions but I don't like the price tag at the supermarket. A jar in the store might cost you £1.50, but when you don the apron and embrace the vinegar, the costs plummet. It takes me no more than 5 minutes to prep the onions and boil the pickling liquor. I do the same for red cabbage and beetroot. All of a sudden you've got ingredients ready to boost any salad. Cheap and incredibly flavourful! I'll stop there before I start telling you about my penchant for pickled fish!

Sharing the Spice of Life

There are a few spices I use which I seem to go through at a very fast rate. Cumin comes to mind. Instead of buying it in small containers from my supermarket over and over again, I buy a kilogram bag at a bulk store. It's £9 for a kilo bag versus the £23 a kilo it ends up costing if I buy from my supermarket. We often forget that a large part of the cost of what we buy is the packaging. Now, I'll probably not use a kilo of cumin before it goes over, so I share some with my friends. It's part of a communal spirit. I'm already saving some money, so why not let my friends benefit, too!

Buy tactically

A whole chicken is so much cheaper than portions. Learn how to break down a chicken and to build cold chicken salad or sandwiches into your meal plan. I buy 10kg bags of rice as rice keeps for a long time and I get the big discount on the big bags. Fillet steak is expensive, but bashing out rump with a rolling pin and voila, it's transformed. Learn how to slow cook cheaper cuts of meat to increase your savings. My point here is that there are usually cheaper alternatives, so look for them and take advantage of them.

Batch cook

Sometimes on a Sunday I'll cook for 2 hours straight. I challenge myself as to how many days worth of food I can cook in that time. Buy lots of tupperware and then box it all up. As a family man with two active children who do every sport going, this is a life saver later in the week when we're short on time. Most people reach for the takeaway menu but my food is already in the fridge cooked from Sunday.

The Health Dividend

While not a direct financial saving, the health benefits of home-cooked meals are apparent. Ready meals, with their high salt, sugar, and fat content, contribute to a myriad of health issues. Cooking at home allows for control over ingredients, ensuring meals are nutritious and tailored to dietary needs. Good health leads to so many financial benefits.

I could go on with a lot more tips but I'll stop there. I feel proud to put meals of nutritious value on the table each day. It's good for the soul, good for everyone's health, and great for the bank account. These tips will hopefully start you on a journey of better habits, or at least make you stop and think. There are many great books and blogs out there to get you started.

Top tips:

- If you're new to cooking then start small. Rome wasn't built in a day and it's the same here. I still have nightmare moments in the kitchen – I'm not a professionally trained chef! My wife will never stop reminding me about the squid in black bean sauce disaster of 2005. (She's never been able to eat black bean sauce since.)
- Some online recipes come with a difficulty rating and the time needed to make them. So if you're a new cook or not feeling confident, then pick things that are quick and easy.
- If you open my kitchen cupboards you'll find all sorts of ingredients. I think I have 4 different types of soya sauce. I've built up an array of ingredients. This makes it super easy to whip up an interesting meal at a moment's notice. But it takes time to build up a pantry to be proud of. Again, start small. Tins of beans, chopped

tomatoes, dried pasta, and other store cupboard essentials are where to start. Keep it simple and have a basic pantry on hand all the time.

To help you here are my top 10 essentials for any kitchen:

1 **Eggs** - practically a ready meal

2 **Plain Flour** - did you say pizza?

3 **Salt and pepper** - add some flavour

4 **Dried Rice** - cooked rice freezes really well

5 **Tinned tomatoes** - one of your 5 a day

6 **Dried Pasta** - long lasting energy

7 **Cold pressed rapeseed oil** - cheaper than olive

8 **Fresh garlic** - more flavour

9 **Dried oregano** - better dried than fresh

10 **Balsamic vinegar** - add to sauces or salad dressing.

THE LOCAL TOUCH

dam, Laura, Graham, Sebastiano, Nicole, Jenn, Lucy, and Belinda. Who are these people?

They are people who work at or own local businesses near me. They are people who have the ability to glue a community together.

Adam is my butcher and he has a lovely old fashioned shop. Adam is a rarity. Not a computer in sight, a traditional till, old-fashioned sawdust on the floor. The pies aren't picture perfect but look like something your Gran would pull out of the oven. While they might not look perfect, their quality soon alleviates any aesthetic concerns.

He keeps his records on paper, he still writes cheques, and he's not great when it comes to using a computer. How much you owe is added up on the paper in which he wraps your meat. But if you visit him on a Saturday morning, there is a queue out the door. Moreover, he's not based in an affluent area, yet the customers arrive in droves.

But how can a business like this survive in a modern commercial environment without the latest technology? Especially when the product doesn't look like the modern perfection we all seem to demand.

It's all about community. In this book, I talk about technology and smart digital tools. But fundamentally, I'm quite a traditional chap who tries to shop locally. I love this idea of community.

Getting back to Adam... His business is a masterclass on how to provide the best customer service. I don't know how many people patronise his business on a weekly basis, but I bet he knows the name of 80% of the people who walk through the door – plus a few facts about their lives and family. And he always has a welcoming smile for everyone who enters his shop.

Wouldn't you like to experience service similar to that at Adam's shop? Where they know by name and care about you? Where they're merely pleased just to see you?

· · ·

I think holding onto community will become more important in the digital age. Businesses like Adam's are hubs of the community. Most services we use tend to be online and, as a result, we're losing our sense of community. But how can a little butcher's shop glue a community together? And what the hell does it have to do with saving 10%!?

The community being developed by this butcher's shop is one of welcome and friendliness. It's one of accessibility to those unable to drive. It's one of social and personal connection – it may even give some customers the only social interaction they will have that day. Small gestures of remembering names and knowing facts about someone's life make a big difference.

I'm just so sick of poor service. It's costing me time and money. On the one hand: Is it really acceptable for me to wait 45 minutes when I have a banking issue? HMRC closed their phone line in January, just before the self-assessment deadline. Phone numbers are disappearing from business websites in favour of what the big corporations all seem to think we want – an AI chatbot!

On the other hand, I recently went into Adam's shop and asked for a shoulder of lamb. He smiled and went to the freezer. He presented to me a bag, upon which was written "Justin." He knew I'd come in asking for one of my family favourites, so he'd put away a good cut for me. Once, when I was ill, he even delivered some meat. And all these feats without the need for a chatbot! In fact, he doesn't even have a website.

Do all his customers get this sort of service? Maybe not. But I go to his shop every week. I never quibble about the price and never complain. I'm just grateful I have access to this outstanding business and all the people working there. Adam is the owner, but it's not just him – his fantastic team also gives the same service and knows customers by name.

In my own business I also strive for exceptional customer service (although I might be biased!). No call queues and, sorry to disappoint you, we only have humans at the end of the phone – no AI chatbots.

When I told one of my colleagues about this chapter, he challenged me: "But Justin, buying locally or using local services is so much more expensive and takes more time."

Is the butcher more expensive than the supermarket? On the face of it, maybe, but let's consider the quality of the product you're buying. When you cook spaghetti bolognese with mince bought from an independent butcher, you will quickly notice a difference. Where is all the water that normally comes out of the meat? There is none, because a proper butcher doesn't inject the meat with water! Many small businesses provide similar types of quality advantages. My local fruit and veg supplier provides a fresh veg box. Yes, it's a touch more expensive but the product is fresher, and the service is plastic free, helping me reduce my carbon footprint.

I buy my insurance from a local broker because it saves time. Jenn or Lucy answers my call, and they know who I am. They understand my needs, which not only saves me time in many ways but also saves me from the delay and frustration of anonymity. The time saving is considerable as they don't make me wait in a call queue for 20 minutes. Time is a commodity that I can't buy more of so a saving like this is priceless. I put a real tangible value on the customer service that businesses give me. The efficiency of local services means that advice is just a phone call away and solutions are tailored to my unique circumstances. This translates into significant time savings and usually a better product.

What about the idea of loyalty? I walked through the door of my local restaurant close to the end of lunch service. One of my meetings had run over. Did they turn me away, or did they instead choose to find me something to eat? Of course they helped me, because loyalty counts for something. I patronise them at least once a week and they helped me out in return.

The same thing happens at my local car repair garage. I don't think I've ever quibbled about their fees, and I've always been friendly and helpful over the years. I think nearly my entire office uses them now. So when my mum's car had a major problem, the garage she took her car to said they couldn't fit her in, despite her needing to be able to transport her grandchildren. But the garage that I patronise had her booked in that very day. She asked how this was possible and the garage replied, "Because your son is an excellent customer of ours." It wasn't because they weren't busy that day (quite the opposite), but they made an exception because I'm loyal.

If you show local businesses loyalty, they will repay you when it counts the most. In times when stress is high, they will come to your aid.

Choosing local is not merely a time-saving strategy. It's a commitment to nurturing the economic health of our community. When I walk into all these local businesses, I'm greeted by familiar faces, people whose lives are interwoven into the fabric of my community. And this personal interaction eliminates impersonal digital barriers – doesn't that sound nice? Finally, keep in mind that some local businesses don't have websites so search them out, they are hidden gems waiting to be found.

The Bigger Picture

This chapter has become more than 10% and I can't even begin to express the savings. In my first book I wrote a whole chapter on time, money, and happiness. My approach of using local business has saved me countless hours and

enriched my life with invaluable relationships and experiences.

Let's remember that the choices we make about where and
how we spend our time can have profound implications not
just for our personal well-being, but for the vitality of our
communities. In the end, time is more about simply saving
it. It's about valuing it, cherishing it, and spending it in ways
that bring joy, connection, and fulfilment.

My belief is that happiness is not found in the accumulation
of wealth but in the richness of our experiences and connec-
tions. It is a principle that guides my decisions, urging me to
choose paths that enhance my own life and those in my
community.

Top tips:

- When looking for a small businesses, it's always a
  good idea to look at the Google Reviews.
- While reviews are a guide, not all hidden gems
  have Google Reviews. Do ask your friends and
  family for recommendations as they'll be keen to
  tell you.
- It takes time to build relationships with local
  businesses. Start asking a few questions when you
  visit. Things like: How long have you worked for the
  business? Is it family owned? What are your
  specialist areas or things you do best? You need to

make an effort to show some interest beyond your own needs. Then you need to visit on a regular basis so your face becomes familiar. All my local favourites receive a Xmas card from me. If you put in the effort, over time they will reward you, and they'll understand what you need even before you do.

6

THE GOOSE THAT LAYS GOLDEN EGGS

The UK tax system is a labyrinth! Did you know there is one UK tax relief scheme so badly understood that it has become the goose that lays golden eggs for HMRC? This particular goose generated £1.3billion in unclaimed tax relief over 5 years! Don't worry I'll tell you all about it later in the chapter.

So where do you start when it comes to savings and tax matters? To begin with, I've written these tips to specifically help people with paid jobs on a payroll scheme. The key to saving money on tax for mere mortals (like myself) is not through complex tax avoidance schemes. I'm not addressing this book to the super-rich but to people like me who work hard and pay tax on their earnings.

I want you to unlock some of the key things you can do to put a few more pounds in your pocket.

. . .

I've included 4 key ideas in the chapter. Two of the ideas are for those who pay tax at 40% and above, and the other two are ideas for those earning less than that. There will be ideas for you no matter your income, as long as you are paying some form of tax on your earnings.

Before I tell you about the four ideas, here are two quick tips to start you off:

Tip #1: While running my accountancy practice, I'm always amazed by how many clients haven't paid attention to their mileage. Paying proper attention to mileage can include things such as creating a file to put travel purchases in, tracking mileage that is specific to business travel, and noting down the number of trips away. If you take care with this type of organisation, you can usually claim all the correct deductions, possibly even VAT where applicable. Even if you're not the owner of a business but an employee, elements of these suggestions can be taken into account. No matter your job position, we all need to be better at our financial admin. While understanding the complex nuances of tax relief and allowances is one thing, we first need to keep accurate and thorough records in order to be able to make all the claims we hope to. Bookkeeping is all about organisation.

Tip #2: Be clear about what is and what isn't an allowable expense. If an expense is wholly and exclusively made in connection with your job or business, then it's usually allowable. For example, a client once asked me if he could tax deduct his haircut. This would definitely be a no because a regular haircut is not needed for any specific function of his job as a finance broker. But if he were a professional dancer then having his hair cut or styled for a performance would become an allowable expense. He would have his regular haircuts, which he couldn't claim, but he would be allowed to claim any haircuts required for any specific function of his job.

Ok, now let's get to my top 4 ideas to help you save:

1. Underpaid mileage

I have a client who gets paid back by his employer at 25p per mile. He does a lot of business miles in his private car, around 20,000 a year. But the HMRC approved allowable mileage rate is 45p on the first 10,000 miles. The employer realised it's too difficult to track employee mileage and to change the allowable rate when the mileage limit is reached. So, the employer has sensibly decided to pay 25p to simplify their business's admin. But does this mean the client has lost the extra 20p of tax relief? No, but the problem is that many people forget to claim it. The employee is entitled to a £2,000 relief on those 10,000 miles. So as a 20% tax payer, that ends up as £400 in cash that HMRC would refund. And double that if you pay tax at 40%. This isn't some tax dodge – it's an allowable deduction. If you are self-assessed, it goes on the tax return. If you're not self-assessed, you just need to fill in a P87 form to request repayments. If you have a company car then the system is slightly different by working off advisory rates. Talk to an accountant if you're unclear. Here is the link to the P87 form. tinyurl.com/42k6zm2j

2. Professional subscriptions & other deductions

Many people have gained professional qualifications and are members of their professional body. Did you know HMRC publishes a list of these bodies where you can reclaim tax on the subscription fees? Just Google "List of approved professional bodies" and it will be first. It's the same as claiming back underpaid mileage allowances. You can use the same P87 form. There are a raft of allowable deductions, such as if you work as a nurse or cabin crew there are allowances for uniform cleaning. Work on a building site and need personal protective equipment (PPE)? Then that's also claimable. Just remember these are expenses where your employer hasn't paid you back and you've had to suffer the cost. HMRC inspectors are reasonable people and these allowances are available to help you and to ensure the economy grows. So make sure you claim the things that you've spent in connection with your job. Please don't use one of those companies who take a cut as it's really easy to do this yourself. If you search my youtube channel at youtube.com/@ask_jt you'll find a video all about the P87 form and how you can claim it. Here is the link: tiryurl.com/jvjx4v49

3. Pension Contributions - the golden egg-laying goose.

At the start of the chapter I quoted an amazing figure. This was from an article in Standard Life which quoted £1.3-billion in underclaimed tax relief from pension contributions over a period of 5 years. Pension tax relief is one of the most misunderstood reliefs available, and it lets HMRC collect all those golden eggs every year.

But I'm just an employee. Should I still read on? Absolutely!

Let me explain the basics by looking at a private pension. If you pay into a private pension your provider will reclaim tax relief on your behalf. You might have seen it on the pension statement. So you've probably thought it's all sorted. Nope! Look carefully at that amount on the statement. If you paid £100 in pension contributions, the tax relief will be £25. But hang on a minute! £25 is neither 20% or 40% of the £100. That's because the £100 was taken from income that had already been taxed, so the amount you have earned, before tax, is £125 (20% of £125 is £25.)

If you are a 40% taxpayer you might be wondering where the other £25 is? Well, the other £25 is in HMRC's bank account waiting for you to make a request for the reclaim. If you are self assessed then you just add it to the tax return. But if you're not self assessed then you actually have to write a letter via the post to reclaim it.

Here is a link to a letter template. tinyurl.com/2bx6dbz2

. . .

Over the course of a year these contributions add up. You can go back 4 years in total including the current tax year to make a request for repayment.

It is worth noting that this does not apply to all pension schemes so do check before you make a claim. If your pension is a "relief at source" pension scheme then you will be able to claim the relief.

4. The Untapped Potential of Gift Aid

I wanted to follow pensions with the topic of gift aid on charitable donations because the same tax relief calculation as described above applies.

Gift Aid stands as a beacon of tax efficiency, yet its potential remains underutilised by many. When a taxpayer donates under Gift Aid, charities can claim an extra 25p for every £1 donated, at no additional cost to the donor. The charity is claiming back the tax you have already paid. Higher-rate taxpayers can claim back the difference between the basic rate of tax the charity reclaims and their rate of tax. This not only amplifies the impact of their donations but also reduces their taxable income.

Example: Let's say a higher-rate taxpayer donates £100 to a charity under Gift Aid. The charity claims an additional £25, making the total donation £125. The donor who pays tax at 40% can claim back the other £25 (£125/20%), effectively reducing the cost of their donation to £75, while the charity benefits from the full £125.

This is why keeping good records is so important. I usually have a raft of clients frantically looking for the donations they made in the tax year when it comes to self assessment time.

Top tips:

- If you fill in your own self assessment then consider an accountant. They will usually highlight and check issues like your pension relief and charitable donations. But not all accountants are brilliant at pointing these things out so maybe you can use this chapter as a conversation starter if you already work with an accountant. An accountant can quickly repay their fees by helping you find allowable reliefs.
- I'm not brilliant at tracking my mileage. But I am very good at adding everything I do to my calendar. This means at the end of the month or year I can produce a mileage report. Recently, I've installed an app called MileIQ which tracks my mileage and saves me the trouble. Wonderful!
- Switching your pension to salary sacrifice can help you if you are close to tax boundaries. More on this in chapter 9.
- Did you know that if you take a colleague with you in the car on a business trip then you get an

extra 5p per mile? This is called an advance passenger payment.

At the time of writing in February 2024 this information was correct so please check the HMRC for details as tax rules change in the Budget. The contents of the chapter are valid for the 23/24 tax year.

7

DEBT: THE NEVER ENDING STORY

*J*ust *to keep the lawyers happy I need to add that I'm not a financial advisor, so consider taking advice before making any significant financial decisions. What might be suitable for me might not always be suitable for your situation or your financial setup. This chapter's aim is to boost your financial education and help you understand debt reduction options.*

I wasn't great at maths at school. You might think that's ironic considering my day job running an accountancy firm. But is it? The maths I learned at school was mostly about concepts that most people don't actually use in the real world. The principles I do understand are the more straightforward things: percentages, addition, multiplication, subtraction, and division. These are the principles I use whilst running my firm, not the complicated concepts I got taught when I was young. Sure, I wasn't great at the tricky stuff when I was at school, and I'm still not. But I don't need it – the maths I use day in and day out are the straightforward principles that we all know. I use them all the time for household bills, debts, and savings. So if I wasn't great at maths in school, so what? Turns out we don't need simultaneous equations in our daily lives!

However...

My clients still constantly complain that although they also learned basic maths in school, they were never taught how to utilise them in effective ways for finding savings, judging investments, and paying off their debts faster.

When I was just 22 I had the opportunity to get on the property ladder. Despite my youth, I understood a few simple concepts. I buy a property, I put some money down as my deposit, and I borrow the rest on a mortgage over 25+ years. The bank makes some money by way of interest and I just pay them back. Simple!

But the banks don't just make some money, they make a <u>lot</u> of money! You see, the banks are harnessing the power of compound interest. Now, compound interest simply uses straightforward concepts that we learned in school. Unfortunately though, most of us weren't taught how these simple concepts turn into compound interest. *Don't panic, I'll break this down so it's easy to understand.*

Let's look at my first house as an example. I borrowed £175,000 at 5% over 25 years. Sounds like a good deal, right? Until I looked in more detail at the mortgage offer. The bank would make £132,000 in interest over the 25 year term! What?! But how and why do they make so much money?

In simple terms, when you make the mortgage payments in the early years, you are paying more interest than capital. The total debt amount is higher, therefore the amount of interest charged by the banks is larger. So in the early stages of the mortgage the bank makes more money.

Let me break it down using a £175,000 mortgage. If you pay the usual monthly mortgage amount every month in the first year of ownership, you only reduce the mortgage capital by £3,571. Yet in the last year of the mortgage, by paying *the same monthly amount* you would reduce the capital by nearly £12,000. Though you pay the same amount in both years (see table below), at the beginning the majority of the payments are going towards the interest, rather than towards the capital.

	Mortgage balance at start of year	Payments made during the year	Interest
Year 1	£175,000	£12,240	£8,669
Year 25	£11,960	£12,240	£327

But what would happen if I paid an extra lump sum on my mortgage on the first day of ownership, before I started making monthly payments? Well, if I paid an extra lump sum of £100 on day one, it turns out that I'd save £250 of interest over the whole term of the mortgage. What would happen if I paid off a further lump sum of £100 on the anniversary of my mortgage every year? Once a year, in other words. Well, without going into the detailed maths, I would save £1580 of interest over the entire term of the mortgage. What if I went even further and paid off an extra lump sum of £100 per *month*? The total interest saved would then be just under £24,000! Yes, you read that correctly, £24,000! That is money that is now in your back pocket rather than in the bank's coffers. And not only do you save on interest, but with any regular overpayments you will also shorten the term of your mortgage. A monthly overpayment of £100 will see you pay off your mortgage a full 4 years earlier than you would've if you'd only paid the minimum payment every month.

Here's the best bit: if your interest rate is higher or your term is longer, the sooner you make an overpayment the better. For example, a 35 year mortgage at 5% on the same £175,000 debt sees the bank making £196,000 in interest. The bank makes more money than the original debt! By the way, if you were to do the monthly overpayment of £100 in this situation, it would result in you saving nearly £51,000 of interest. Wow!

Fortunately, most mortgages have the option to make overpayments (up to a certain annual limit), but do check your terms and conditions just to make sure.

. . .

All this similarly applies to your savings, but in reverse. If you put £100 into a savings account that pays 5% interest, you would receive £250 in interest at the end of 25 years. The interest in the first year would only be £5.13, but in the last year it would be around £17. That's because interest is earned on the interest that was earned in the earlier years. So the longer you can keep your money in savings, the more money you will get in return. Whether it be mortgage debt or savings, this premise of interest being earned on interest is fundamentally called compound interest.

The principles I've just described are also effective for other types of debt such as loans, car finance, and credit cards.

To illustrate this point let me tell you about my car. About a year ago I needed to buy a replacement car urgently due to a major breakdown. I found a car but I'd not yet had a chance to sell the old car. As I was in a rush, I agreed to take the dealer's finance of 10.9%. I knew the finance was expensive but the terms and conditions allowed unlimited overpayments...and I had a plan. As soon as I sold my old car I used the funds to pay a chunk off the finance, which saved £5,900 of interest straight away. I then contacted my bank and arranged a loan at a much lower rate of 5%. I still needed to pay interest on the new loan but the savings in interest between the two rates was about £6,770. The key point is that an overpayment, made early when the rate is high, will dramatically push down the overall cost of the borrowing.

. . .

The message here is clear: a monthly minimum payment might seem convenient but overpaying and restructuring can save you thousands of pounds in the long run.

Consider a credit card balance of £5,000 with an annual interest rate of 19.9%. If you were to make only the minimum payment, typically set at around 2.5% of the remaining balance or £5 (whichever is higher), it would take nearly 32 years to clear the debt. And you'd pay more than £7,400 in interest!

Just like with mortgage debt, the principle of overpaying applies to credit card debts, too. Paying more than the minimum payment can drastically reduce the total interest cost and repayment term. For example, increasing the monthly payment on a £5,000 credit card debt from the minimum payment up to £200 could reduce the repayment term from over three decades to around 34 months. Of course, there'd also be a significant reduction in total interest paid.

Another idea to consider is the consolidation of debts using a loan that has a much lower interest rate than the ones you currently pay. Consolidating a £5,000 credit card debt that has a very high interest rate using a loan that has a 5% interest rate would see the debt quashed in around 26 months. But keep in mind to speak to a professional before doing so.

· · ·

Finally, I recommend you prioritise paying off credit card debts first. The first step towards financial freedom involves formulating a plan to tackle high interest rate debts as soon as you can.

A quick way to assess which interest rates are hurting you the most is the rule of 72. If you put 72 into a calculator and divide by the interest rate it tells you (roughly) how quickly the bank will double their money. For example, an interest rate of 5% sees the bank doubling their money in 14.4 years (72 divided by 5). In terms of a credit card interest rate of 19.9%, the bank doubles their money in just 3.6 years (72 divided by 19.9). The rule of 72 can also be applied to savings or investments to tell you how quick you can double your own money.

Top tips:

- Regularly review your mortgage. If your fixed rate is coming to an end, shop around for a new deal. Avoid the lender's standard variable rate as these tend to be worse than agreeing a fixed rate or tracker deal.
- Always check the terms and conditions. As much as I encourage overpayments, some institutions will make you pay an "early repayment charge." You want to avoid these, and they can be hidden in the fine print. Early repayment charges can quickly offset the benefits of making the overpayments.

- Talk to an independent mortgage advisor or debt planner if you are stuck. These people are great at what they do.
- If you are tight on cash and can't make significant overpayments or lump sum payments, try simply rounding up your debt payments. For example, if you are paying £570 a month for a mortgage then go to £600. It may seem like a small increase, but it might save you upward of £7,000 over 25 years.
- Keep your credit record in good order as this will mean you get the best rates. Talk to someone qualified early if you are struggling, before you start missing payments.
- When times are good, make overpayments. If you've made overpayments but then later run into financial difficulty, you'll be in a much better position.

8

IT'S ELECTRIFYING

I talked about smart heating controls earlier in the book to help with our gas bill, but what about electricity?

January usually brings me a horrifying electricity bill! This year was no exception, with the bill weighing in at 250 pounds.

Most of us spend at least £1,000 a year on electricity, representing a considerable cost to many households. For others like me, it can be so much more.

My electricity is so significant because we have two electric cars. We're an active family doing a raft of sports, so the washing machine never stops. The tumble dryer has a hard life trying to keep up with our sporting garments. Plus, the dishwasher must be on twice a day.

.   .   .

In the UK, electricity represents around 13% of an average household's total energy costs for the year. With our busy family and two electric cars, I find our own bill is about 40%.

Cutting down on electricity can involve a wide range of solutions, from simple, low-cost strategies all the way up to technology that costs thousands of pounds. The UK government wants to change the country's energy mix from gas and oil to electricity, so our electricity overhead will inevitably grow. So, action today will put you in good stead for the future.

A Note on Electric Cars

Before I get into my electrifying advice, I want to mention electric cars. I could probably write a whole chapter on electric vehicles, but I'm not sure I would find 10% savings. However, I mention electric cars in several places in this chapter, so I must address this elephant in the room. I believe electric cars are one of the last things you should consider when trying to save money. Address other areas first. The large capital outlay of an electric car makes me wonder how much money can be saved. My last second-hand electric car depreciated £17,000 in less than a year. When facing such fast depreciation rates, it's hard to justify the upfront costs. But we still own two electric cars and they do cost much less on fuel and maintenance, so I still believe in them. In this chapter I discuss ideas about how we can control our EV charging rates, and in the next chapter I revisit how you can bring down the costs of electric vehicles. You'll likely own an electric car at some point in the not-too-distant future, so I don't want this chapter to provide information yet leave you wondering why I didn't tell you about electric vehicles.

So, let's get into my quick-fire tips to slash your electricity:

Small Changes

Before you spend money on energy-saving products, get back to basics. Change your fridge temperature to 5 degrees and ensure the freezer is no lower than -18 degrees. Make sure your freezer is full, it's more efficient when full. But don't overfill your fridge, because you need to allow for cool air circulation. Once fully charged, don't leave your electronic devices plugged in. Put a lid on your pan when cooking. Turn off devices at the switch so they aren't on standby mode. Use small appliances for cooking, such as slow cookers, air fryers, and pressure cookers. Only run the dishwasher when it is full. Develop good habits for turning off lights. Replace lightbulbs with LEDs. Do your washing on a 30-degree wash (you'll be amazed at how well this works). Turn down the TV and computer brightness. The little things really can make a big difference.

Appliances

Begin by assessing your most energy-intensive appliances and prioritise replacing them. You don't need to be scientific about finding power-hungry appliances. Just ask Google, and a list will appear. If you have a smart meter, check your energy monitor to understand what is using power and when. If one of these power-hungry appliances breaks, invest a bit more money in one that is more energy efficient and of better quality. In my case, the tumble dryer emerged as the top energy consumer. To address this, I invested in an advanced tumble dryer with heat pump technology. This type of dryer is notably more energy-efficient than models with traditional electric heating elements. The new dryer also has an extended warranty for added peace of mind. It can seamlessly integrate with my solar power system, activating when excess solar energy is available, which further optimises electricity use and reduces costs. I found that replacing mine did yield a valuable saving on electricity costs.

Dehumidifiers

Using a dehumidifier can be beneficial not just for saving money on electricity but also for saving on your overall household energy bills. First, it removes moisture from the air, facilitating more efficient room heating, resulting in reduced heating costs. Second, air drying damp laundry near a dehumidifier significantly speeds up air drying, offering a cost-effective alternative to a tumble dryer, especially in the winter months when the good old British weather means drying inside the home is the only option. However, it's not practical to have a dehumidifier in every room. It's best to strategically place it in areas where you typically hang laundry to dry or areas that require more frequent heating. This approach ensures optimal utilisation of the dehumidifier. They can be helpful in older houses (like mine) where dampness is an issue.

Overnight charging rates & intelligent tariffs

We have a smart energy tariff. Firstly, I get a cheap energy rate which is 74% cheaper for 6 hours overnight than during the rest of the day. This type of energy tariff is perfect for charging our electric cars as we can set them to charge only during the reduced rate timeframe. Not only do I charge my car, but I can also programme my dishwasher, dryer, and washing machine to come on during the low-cost window. I can take even more advantage of the cheap energy period by charging my solar battery during these off-peak hours. I can then use that stored energy during high-peak hours, instead of drawing from the grid at those more expensive times. There was also a brief period recently where the overnight charge rate was lower than the gas rate. I used this opportunity to heat my hot water tank. A water tank is an excellent way of storing energy if you don't have a solar system setup with a battery. Sometimes, these electric tariffs are called EV charging tariffs. One forward-thinking energy company even offers an intelligent tariff that detects when an electric car is plugged in. As the electric car can connect to the internet it talks to the energy company. If spare energy is available in the grid, it's possible to top up the car at a cheaper rate, outside the usual overnight cheap rate, without even lifting a finger!

Solar Panels

I could write an entire chapter on solar panels, but I have decided to provide only a selection of ideas instead, because solar is an expensive option. If you'd like further detailed information on the cost-saving benefits of solar panels after you finish reading the chapter, there are two places you can go:

1 In my other book, The Science of Business, I wrote a chapter called Going Green, which looks at my solar output in greater detail.

2 I have a free e-learning course called "Going Green," which explains in detail how our home solar system works. You can find the course at AskJT.co.uk.

So, are solar panels worth it? My home has a solar panel system with battery storage which I got professionally installed in 2018. I started this chapter by quoting my January electricity bill of £250. But January is always the worst for sunlight, the fuel for solar panels. For each of the summer months, I only paid around £65 per month, despite the soaring inflation in energy costs last year. And don't forget we also have two electric cars and a very energy-intensive lifestyle!

As far as the cost of installing a solar panel system goes, I asked my friend Chris to share his recent solar quotation. He'd asked a company to quote on installing panels, so here are some up to date costs. (I installed my panels quite a while ago.) He would have to pay just over £10,000 for a 3.87kw system with a battery. The system indicated a saving of £710 a year (a 7.1% return).

Here are some more ideas to help you optimise and save.

Optimising your system further:

- For my friend, the solar quotation he received showed that in four months out of twelve, he'd generate more solar energy than he could consume. Fortunately, he has an electric car, because it's possible to use an electric car as a secondary battery. In short, your car battery is a way of storing spare solar power. When you connect your car to the house it is usually drawing power from the grid. When you have a solar system installed there is a special device called an inverter which regulates power from the panels and battery. In most home solar setups, the inverters can only deliver power to the house at a maximum of 3.6kw, but car chargers deliver around 7kw. This difference means some electricity still has to be bought from the grid. But some electric cars allow you to turn down the amps at which the car draws power. You can effectively charge your car below the inverter threshold. Imagine going to the petrol station and not having to pay for fuel. Free miles!
- What about your water tank if you don't have an electric car to take spare energy? Water is a great way to store energy, so installing a solar diverter can be a great addition. A diverter is a special device that detects when your solar battery is full and therefore directs the spare energy to go into your water tank, rather than being left unused.

- Check the weather forecast before leaving the house and delay starting when your main appliances, like the dishwasher, turn on. I want my solar battery to be full by the time my appliances draw power, so that they draw from the excess solar energy being generated *after* the battery can no longer accept it. I don't want that excess energy going to waste. I want to be the one using the energy when my system generates surplus — it would be directed to the grid otherwise. In the summer months, my solar battery can be full by 11am on a sunny day, so I use the delay start feature to time my appliances to spring to life after that time.

- Don't forget you can charge your solar battery overnight using your smart energy tariff, if you have one. Once you have the infrastructure, you can start to take advantage of these other areas too.

Part own a Wind Farm.

Don't have the room for a solar system? There is a company called Ripple Energy that lets you invest in part of a wind farm. Once you invest in a wind farm project, this wind farm (once built) generates income. It is this income which is used to offset your energy bill. When you get your bill there will be an extra line for income that reduces the overall cost. You may need to move to a compatible energy supplier who can accept the wind farm income, but some people have offset their bill beyond 100%. You may also need to wait a while as there is a waiting list to access new wind projects, and they may need to be constructed. But it's a wonderful idea. Don't forget that you are buying a type of investment, so seek financial advice before doing something like this.

Top tips:

- The companies selling solar solutions offer finance, but please be careful. Don't take finance over long periods. Anything beyond five years is madness, in my opinion. I saw one deal running into 15 years at 11.29%. Suddenly, a £10,000 system would cost around £21,000 in the long run. If you need to take finance, it will affect any overall return. Seek financial advice before taking on finance.
- Don't rush into expensive options until you understand how much energy you use.
- Look for grants, especially if you receive state or disability benefits.
- If you are investing in energy solutions, get a few quotes and check out the reviews. Sometimes, the cheapest option isn't the best.

9

SACRIFICE SOME SALARY

One of my clients received a pay rise last year, from £50,000 to £55,000 per annum. They were pleased with their recent promotion but their mean accountant (me) was soon to burst this short-lived bubble.

> *"As you have two children, you'll need to pay an extra £942 in tax and complete a self-assessment tax return," I said.*

I'd dropped the bombshell that the client would need to start repaying their child benefit.

"But my wife only works part-time; she only earns £20,000 per annum. Childcare is so expensive, so she can't work full time." The client was angry.

·   ·   ·

The client hadn't realised the change in the "effective tax rate." Effective tax is the average rate of tax we pay on all our earnings. I don't want to bog you down with calculations, so here are the critical numbers for this example:

The payrise was £5,000. The tax, national insurance, and child benefit bill, just on the extra £5000, totalled £3,013. That is an effective tax rate of around 60.3%! The client had also moved to a point where tax at 40% was becoming due.

"There was no point in me getting the pay rise! Why the hell are middle-class people paying 60% tax?!"

The client had posed a question which is a political hot potato and often posed to me.

Fortunately, I had a solution up my sleeve.

"Does your employer offer salary-sacrificing options for pension contributions? What about an electric car salary-sacrifice scheme?"

There are some danger thresholds regarding the UK tax system: those who repay child benefit and those earning over £100,000 per annum. If you repay child benefit, you can quickly find yourself paying taxes above 60%. When earnings reach £100,000, you start to lose your personal allowance, resulting in another 60% effective tax rate. Maybe it's time to dig out your payslip and check your income level?

Shortly before publishing this book, the March Budget of 2024 announced a change in the rules on child benefit. This sometimes happens when you write about tax. While the threshold for child benefit repayment has been raised to £60,000, my points about salary sacrifice are still valid to manage tax thresholds. The new rules on child benefit will make the tax rate less extreme, but it will still be around 50%. Plus, the problem of a 60% effective tax rate above £100,000 still exists.

The key message to this chapter is that my suggestions for salary sacrifice will work no matter your income threshold (as long as you are paying some tax). If you are a 20% taxpayer, then you save 20% tax, if 40% then it's 40%. But if you are in one of the danger points like earning more than £60,000 or £100,000, then your savings could be up to 60%.

Going back to my client, who had drifted into paying 40% tax and repaying some of their child benefit, what advice would I give?

Salary sacrifice & Non-cash benefits

My first port of call is usually salary sacrifice arrangements. These involve agreeing to exchange a portion of your salary for non-cash benefits. These non-cash benefits can lead to substantial savings in income tax and national insurance contributions. This arrangement benefits employers and employees by reducing the tax liabilities for both parties. But what is a non-cash benefit?

Non-cash benefits are when you give up part of your salary in exchange for something like a mobile phone, a company car, pension contributions, private medical cover, etc.

Some of these benefits, like private medical insurance, attract what are called Benefits in Kind (BIK), which are taxable. But I'm interested in telling you about the non-cash benefits that reduce taxes.

Salary Sacrifice Pensions

If you're employed, you're probably contributing to a pension. But sometimes you can opt to give up part of your salary in exchange for the employer making your pension contribution instead of you. *The same amount is still being paid into your pension*, but your employer is now making *the contribution* all on your behalf. Sounds like an insignificant change, doesn't it?

But it's not. If you earn £55,000 but are contributing, say £150 a month as your employee contribution, your salary is still stated as £55,000. With salary sacrifice, your employer lowers your salary by £1,800 per annum and then contributes to the pension. The pension deduction line disappears or might be shown differently. In the case of my client who receives child benefit, this would save around

60% on £1,800, which is over £1000 of tax saving. It's an excellent method to lower you out of 40% tax thresholds or if you are just over the £100,000 earnings threshold as well.

Topping up a private pension

Unfortunately, in the example above, my client's employer didn't offer a salary sacrifice option. So he sensibly decided to pay some extra money into his private pension.

He paid £4,000 into his private pension; the pension company recovered tax at 20%, and he recovered tax at 20%. The significant benefit is that suddenly he gets to keep all of his child benefit.

So, rather than me asking him to pay £942 via self-assessment, he now got a <u>refund</u> of £946. He saved £1,888 on his self-assessment. Don't forget that he has already paid some tax via employment.

Of course, this idea only works if you have a spare £4,000 to invest in a pension. But even if someone couldn't pay the full amount, each £100 in cash they introduce to the pension saves £63 (when they have child benefit and breach the 40% tax threshold.)

It's not just people in these danger thresholds but anyone paying 40% tax who may wish to reduce some of their tax. A pension contribution has the effect of increasing something called your basic rate band. In short, less of your income is due at 40%, but remember to reclaim your tax relief. See chapter 6.

Electric Car Salary Sacrifice

Some employers offer employees the ability to take on an electric car by sacrificing some pension. Currently, the government is encouraging tax breaks on electric vehicles as part of our race to carbon net zero.

I have a client who had a situation where he was paying £750 a month in car finance payments, insurance, tax, maintenance and fuel. But he suddenly discovered he could take a salary sacrifice car from his employer for less than he was currently paying monthly. Simply put, the employer pays for the vehicle and deducts the cost from his salary. So rather than paying for the vehicle after tax, he paid before. Taking the car via salary sacrifice moved this particular client out of the situation where he lost his personal allowance to one where he regained it. It was a 60% reduction in tax!

But isn't there some tax to pay? Yes, there is a small Benefit in Kind (BIK) tax to pay for electric cars. I own an electric vehicle which costs about £50,000. The BIK on this car is 2%. So I have £1,000 benefit, and then I need to pay tax, usually at 40% on this £1000. But £400 in tax for a £50,000 car is exceptional value.

·   ·   ·

Allowable Expenses

I talked earlier in the book about allowable expenses. If you have underpaid mileage or charitable donations, this will extend your basic rate (20%) tax threshold. Thinking back to my earlier chapter, I talked about someone being owed £2,000 in relief for underpaid mileage. In my example of the client with the £5,000 pay rise, he'd now only be affected by the repayments on £3,000 of his earnings. It's always worth checking those allowable expenses and claiming where allowances are available.

Cycle to Work Scheme

The Cycle to Work scheme is a brilliant initiative that promotes eco-friendly commuting while providing financial benefits. Employees can acquire bicycles and safety equipment through their employer, paid back through salary sacrifice, resulting in savings on tax. Again, this works well to lower you out of difficult points in tax thresholds.

Top Tips:

- Another aspect of salary sacrifice schemes in the UK is childcare vouchers which, despite being phased out, offer ongoing benefits for those already enrolled. These vouchers allow parents to pay for childcare from their pre-tax salary, offering significant savings.
- If you are a 40% taxpayer and reaching a point where you will retire, it could be a good idea to increase your contributions to your pension. The increase in pension allows you to save 40% tax. In

the not-too-distant future, you can get a 25% tax-free lump sum when you draw your pension. Speak to your financial advisor or accountant if this might benefit you.

- I hope this chapter has given you the skills to identify opportunities to take advantage of relief. The contents of this chapter are complex, so use skilled professionals to help you.

A final word on salary sacrifice. While the advantages are clear, it's crucial to consider the potential impact on pension entitlements, maternity pay, and loan applications, as salary sacrifice can reduce your official taxable income. A balanced approach is essential, considering both immediate benefits and long-term implications.

At the point of writing and publishing this book, the advice given above is correct. The change in legislation was announced in March 2024 and changed from 6th April 2024. I therefore had not had the chance to read the guidance notes in full, which is why I've not changed my example. I will aim to provide an updated chapter towards the end of 2024 for those reading this as an e-book.

MIND OVER MACHINE

T he development of this book tested my skills and knowledge of automation, cloud technology, and AI. But it also put my own personal drive and motivation to the test. You see, I started writing the book on February 5th. Then, just 12 days later, I announced the date of the book launch. There was no going back!

Spurred into action, I had my editor working on the first chapters by the 20th of February. To hit my ambitious time-line, I needed to upload the manuscript to Amazon's Kindle platform by March 14th, so the pressure was on. In the end, I finished writing on the 4th of March. I had completed the book in less than 30 days.

My last book, "The Science of Business," took me eight months to complete, while many other business authors spend years writing their masterpieces. But 30 days for a whole book, Justin, you must be mad! But it was indeed possible – what you're reading is testament to that. I did it by using smart digital skills and with only a limited budget.

The book came to life because of a speaking event I was doing for bestselling author, Michael Heppell. He'd asked me to do a talk called "10 Ideas to Save 10% in 10 minutes". I was to deliver the talk on the 17th of February and, like all good professional speakers, I did my homework. I laid out 10 points and fleshed out a script. And then, as I looked at my final script two weeks prior to the speaking event, I thought, "I wonder if I could turn this into a book...and be confident enough to announce that book's release at the speaking event!?"

So...

I had ISBNs left over from my first book project, a paid subscription of ChatGPT, and access to all sorts of other software. Along with the script, I fed a brief of around 150 words into ChatGPT. I then asked it to generate a book outline and some sample content. Please remember that it was all my own ideas and thoughts that were the foundation for the script. By using ChatGPT I was merely looking for a helping hand to start.

The content that ChatGPT developed was different from my personal writing style, but it gave me stuff to work with. It showed me some things I'd not necessarily thought of that could be expanded upon to help me communicate my own ideas. While I was creating my first book, Michael Heppell would often say to me, "Write shite.' The mantra simply means that a writer should just get words, any words, down on the page. Fortunately, ChatGPT took care of that horrible "write shite" stage for this book. (A stage that took me several weeks to complete for my first book.) Thanks to ChatGPT, I had an outline and some basic structure, plus suggestions for chapter headings. Most of those chapter titles have changed (except this chapter, which I retained in order to make a point), but I had that all-important head start. Don't worry. Nothing that ChatGPT created remains, but my point is this: technology has advanced, and I wasn't afraid to use it. It helped me develop a whole book in just over a month!

Much more goes into writing a book than just putting words on the page. I used Grammarly to suggest better sentence structure and correct spelling errors. I used another app to judge the reading age of each chapter and identify hard-to-read sentences. I used typesetting software where I uploaded a file and a beautifully formatted book (that was print and e-book ready) came out the other end. I used templates from Canva to build the cover design. I used a Google Doc to collaborate with my editor, Steven. He was able to edit each chapter as I completed it, rather than waiting for the whole book to be finished. By the time I had finished writing the book, the chapters were nearly fully edited.

I used an innovation principle called lean startup, part of which involved looking at the resources I already had at hand. I didn't need to buy new resources, rather I was able to repurpose them. Multitasking isn't always my strong point, so using collaborative software tools was able to cut down the book's development time.

My marketing was even semi-automated. I used a social media management tool. I recycled content I'd developed in the past that could be reposted. Did you know a social post only has a useful life of a few hours? There is nothing wrong with reusing "good" content again in the future. It takes time to develop social content, so why not reuse it again? Every social post I added created a library which could be reused and automatically scheduled for future use. I had a highly engaged email marketing list that could be used to drive initial interest in the book on launch day.

Most importantly though, it was technology that was vital in reducing my book writing from potentially years to just over a month. It's not all about AI, not even close, but instead about harnessing a remit of digital skills.

I'm not here to teach you how to become an AI expert or even how to write a book, but rather to open your eyes to what technology has to offer. If you can become a technology master, the efficiency savings are waiting.

Automation is a subject about which I'm more excited than AI. AI tools like ChatGPT are wonderful, but they can't always complete my tasks. The output from AI software often needs lots of work, and we can't always know if it's accurate. But it's the world of automation that gives me quick wins every day with very little human input.

What is automation? I've already discussed smart heating controls in another chapter, and they are a great example. You leave the house and the heating switches off. It's simple automation: The heating app detects you have left the house, so it switches off.

My Alexa is programmed to tell my children when it's time for breakfast and to even switch off the TV. And just how helpful do you think it is that Alexa also reminds my forgetful eldest child, James, to go catch the bus?!

We all own gadgets of some kind that we use in our personal lives, and we should learn how to effectively use them to automate the mundane.

But what about in our work lives?

When I meet a new prospective client, our business needs to send a proposal (basically just a quotation). We use a clever piece of software that integrates our pricing, terms and conditions, and digital signatures all into one place. It's great! But we still have to plan all the work, raise invoices, enter data into a CRM, save client files, etc. The list is endless. It is the same for many businesses. However, in my business, everything I've just mentioned is automated.

. . .

For example, our proposal software has done a great job of eliminating the need to create engagement letters (our terms and conditions). We no longer need to create letters with separate word processing software, and we no longer need to upload such letters into separate e-signature software. However, the proposal software can only do so much. It's limited by its specific purpose.

What about all the other things we need to get done every day? Wouldn't it be helpful if all sorts of data could be seamlessly moved to our accounting software? Could it be useful to utilise practice management software and time tracking software? Is there software that could raise an invoice? Something to automatically allocate work assignments to members of staff? Could we track down files that had been sent via email and automatically store them in correct client folders in our cloud storage system?

The answer to each is Yes! My business does all these things, and they all happen *automatically*. Last month, over 600 tasks were completed through automation.

Here is a list of all the steps that automation takes care of when we take on a new client:

- Client accepts proposal
- Client created in accounting software
- Raising upfront invoice

- Direct debit sign-up link
- Client record created in our practice management system
- Job created in our practice management system
- Client record created and resulting data moved into CRM
- Slack message sent via our new client channel to inform entire team
- Client and project created in our time-tracking system
- File located, folder created, and file saved to cloud storage
- Client added to email drip campaign
- Handover letter to prior accountant created from template

How does all this magic happen? It all started with our proposal software as a kick-off point, but that software didn't have the capacity to integrate with all our other bits of software.

So we now use a piece of software called Zapier. It allows me to create "Zaps" that can automate parts of my business without writing a single line of code. For instance, a Zap connects all sorts of other software, such as saving email attachments to Dropbox or posting notifications in Slack. This saves precious time and reduces the need for manual intervention, and it provides greater consistency while reducing potential errors.

. . .

I mentioned that our new clients are put on an email drip campaign, a campaign that includes a lot of educational information. They get around 40 emails from us per year, and the best bit is that they get added to the list automatically. I never have to remember to press the Send button.

I could write a whole book on the things contained in this chapter, but for now I simply want to inspire you to find technology solutions that will help you work smarter, not harder.

Check out my automation webinar on my YouTube channel if you want to learn more.

Top tips:

- Find out where staff members are entering data from one system into another. Can this be automated?
- Listen to clients who repeatedly ask the same question. We try to build these answers into our email education so we don't have to answer them so often.
- Purchase invoice processing is low-hanging fruit. Did you know tasks like this can be outsourced to software like Dext and Hubdoc. They magically read the data for you and input it into accounting software.
- Get your smartphone and smart devices configured to automate the mundane parts of your life.
- Don't underestimate the challenge of setting up this type of automation. It does require time and dedication to get it right, but the rewards are worth it.

BONUS: SAVINGS HACKS FROM MY FRIENDS

I decided to ask my social media community for their best ideas for saving time and money. This book is about 10% savings, but there are loads of other ways to save. So, I thought I'd publish some of the brilliant ideas from my followers.

Ask Justin to help you decorate. (My friend hit the nail on the head that it's cheaper to ask friends to help you with DIY.) **Robert Stewart**

Check for any unused subscriptions and software you've forgotten about and cancel them. **Stephen Pardue**

Buy a large second hand freezer. Batch cook and fill meals with lots of cheap meals. **Debbie Homer-Davis**

. . .

Learn a new skill so you don't have to pay someone to do it for you. There isn't too much out there that's so difficult that it stops you from giving it a whirl. There is a video on YouTube for practically anything. **Andrew Burnip**

Ask for a discount. If they say no, you're exactly where you were. If they say yes... You'll never make money faster than when you're saving it. **Bill Heppell**

Grocery shopping. Find the time your local supermarket does the price reduction. You can pick up food for pence. **Dawn Booth**

I always buy second-hand books now, even as gifts. Good for the wallet and the environment, and you can buy more of them. In the garden, I love making free plants by propagating and dividing. We always give away spider plants and suchlike in our kid's party bags. **James Pocock**

Buy toiletries in bulk and decant into smaller bottles. **Jacqueline Winnell**

Try Olio, it takes discount, best before food to the next level. **Michael Heppell**

. . .

Rotate Streaming services. Exhaust one then replace it with another instead of having them all at once. **Steven Holmberg**

Earn it before you spend it. **Andrew Bettany**

Upcycle existing furniture instead of buying new. **Eleanor Baggaley**

Make money from what you've already bought. We sometimes buy things we never use – certainly women do this with clothes – or use them only once or twice. Pre-loved is very popular. Obviously, eBay and Vinted are great apps. I made over £2,000 last year from items I had in the house that I'd never worn or had only used a few times. **Sarah McGeough**

I rarely buy my son new clothes. We use Facebook Marketplace whenever we can, and while he was still little all his toys were from FB Marketplace too, including baby accessories like buggies and cots. **Andrea Sandu**

I was taught to get my clothes to at least £1 per wear. Although I taught the kids 10p per wear. How many people buy something and wear it once, but it costs £5 OR you spend £120 and wear it regularly for 5 years. **Geordie Gill**

. . .

Don't be fooled by branding. Most baked beans and a range of other products taste pretty much the same! Do a blind taste test and if you can't pick out the branded version, why pay the extra? **Sally Louise**

Repair rather than renew if possible, and don't pay more than you have to. **Noel Wincote**

I'm always telling people to review their paid subscriptions. Quite often everything they need is on the free version. Great examples are Canva, LinkedIn, and most social media scheduling tools. **Dave Rogers**

Challenge yourself to have no general waste, recycling, or food waste for collection. You'll find you save a fortune and discover where you waste money. **Sally Betts**

Buy what you need...not what you want! **Rosee Elliott**

Never go food shopping when hungry and stick to what is on your food plan. The bill at the till is always cheaper. **Greg O'Connell**

I love the App "Too good to go." Very good value for money and sometimes you get loads! I like the surprise of it! **Nicola James**

. . .

Organise your kitchen so the most frequently used items are near where you have the dishwasher. This saves loads of time when you are unloading. **Susan Turner**

Use AI for simple time consuming tasks. I created an informational text for my students and translated it into 4 different languages. It took about 10 minutes. **James Kaunhoven**

Accept that simply getting things done is better than trying to get everything perfect. Outsource what you can, like cleaning and DIY. Combine activities together like taking the kids to school with a shopping trip. **Samantha Lawrence**

Meal Plan. Use up all ingredients, even if it means making soup and then freezing it for lunches. **Emma Burnip**

Visit Facebook groups about 'FIRE' – short for Financial Independence, Retire Early. While some of the groups are more about specific ways to live off of owning rental property or stock investments, there are good tips for saving in there too, and sometimes even adopting a certain mindset helps a lot in actually finding the options that are staring you in the face. **Allan Høiberg**

For a recent project, I rescued some timber from the timber yard skip (with their ok). Someone else had some flooring they were taking to the skip left over from their own project. My project cost me nothing but the screws and shelf brackets. **Jayne N Mark**

Put your money in a savings account. It depends on your time horizon, appetite for risk, etc. But for most people right now, you can already beat the UK's 4% inflation rate by putting your money in a savings account with around 5% interest. **Robert Pearce**

Use PIR sensor switches in your toilet/bathrooms, especially if you have kids. **Chris McConnell**

Do you use your gym membership, or could you buy some equipment and exercise at home? **Nicky Whatley**

Never go food shopping when you're hungry. You'll buy all sorts of rubbish if you do. **Catherine Cliffe**

Why drive or walk when you can get on your Bike? I cut down toothpaste at the end to get more before it's thrown away. We save seed heads for next year. Make your own cards. I get my new clothes from charity shops and look for new labels. **Di Parker**

· · ·

Follow the 2 minute rule - unless you are really busy. If you have a specific task that will take less than 2 minutes, just do it in the moment, don't put it off. **Fiona Nash**

I adjusted some of the wording in the comments to make them easier to read, but they are true to what people left in my social media comments. Thank you to everyone who left a comment.

SAMPLE FROM THE SCIENCE OF BUSINESS

If you enjoy this sample then consider buying my other book from Amazon it's called the The Science of Business.

Just visit www.thescienceofbusiness.co.uk and it will take you to my Amazon page. Plus don't forget to leave a review. This is the first half of chapter 7, I hope you enjoy it.

7. The Injured Deer - Everyone is different

"Are you better working individually or in a team?"

I hate this question! Interviewers ask this question but have no idea why they are asking it. Neither the person asking the question nor the person answering it really understands.

You see, I'm an extrovert, so I need people around me to give me my mental energy. That interview question should exist in order to determine a personality type. Sorry, but the vast majority of us just don't have the foggiest. I'm 39 and it is only in the last 5 years I could have made a reasonable attempt at answering the question effectively. That said, I would have been safe anyway, as the interviewer wouldn't have understood why they were asking the question in the first place.

Now bear with me. I'm not going to tell you about magic crystals or the power of the sun giving us superpowers. I'm a man of science, after all, and this chapter will help you understand how your brain works. It will help you to understand others.

Before I start my story, I want you to do something for me. Cross your fingers or your arms. Now try to do it the opposite way. Doesn't that feel odd! Your brain has been wired in a particular way and it prefers doing things in that way. Here is another one: look in a mirror and move your eyes side to side. I'll bet you don't see anything. That's because your brain has filtered out the movement. Your brain is merely making guesses most of the time and then filling in the gaps.

So what does all this mean, and what can we do about it?

My Story of Discovery

Through a networking group, I was offered the opportunity to do a Myers-Briggs test, and about a dozen of us decided to team up. Since we'd clubbed together we were able to secure a great deal for a normally expensive exercise. Included were the test, results, 1-to-1 psychologist assessments, and a follow up training day. A tester came to the office and administered the test to me. The test scores were added up and we were given our results. Terrific, I thought, a load of letters – I was apparently an ESTJ. If I'm being honest, I had been a little sceptical about the whole thing, but little did I know a life changing experience was about to follow.

Next up was a psychologist who came to my office and asked me even more questions. Here's where things became fascinating. She gave me several insights into my personality, including the fact that, although the test measured me as well-organised, in actuality I do not tend to be adept at organisation skills. It's only because my powers of self-control and professional training overcome this tendency to disorganisation that I test as well-organised.

"You're not naturally well organised," she said.

Bang! She was on the money. I use diaries, project management software, lists, etc. to keep myself organised. So my Myers-Briggs result was changed by the psychologist from ESTJ to ESTP. During the same meeting, a question popped into my brain and I blurted it out.

"My wife thinks I'm dead inside as I never cry at films. Am I?"

"Why do you say that?" she asked, laughing.

I explained that I'd recently watched the film *Boy in the Striped Pyjamas* and not a tear was in sight. Through her own flood of tears my wife cried, "There is something wrong with you, you're dead inside!"

Her comment had been bothering me ever since. I could empathise with the horrible things portrayed on screen, but they couldn't bring me to tears.

"Of course you're not dead inside. In fact, it's completely normal for your personality type, and I can prove it. Your brain is wired more than most others to interpret facts. You score highly on the Myers-Briggs scale in this area. The 2nd World War happened a long time ago so your brain simply tells you there is nothing you can do to change the outcome. Moreover, you're watching a film – your brain perceives a fictional story and finds it hard to relate it to real life. You feel there's simply nothing you can do in the present to help those poor people and the boy in the striped pyjamas."

Wow! This was mind blowing, and there was still more to come..............

Read the rest of the chapter by buying The Science of Business.

ACKNOWLEDGEMENTS

To my long-suffering wife Sue. I often used you in my storytelling form of writing. Despite all the stories, I do love you to the moon and back. Sue declared after I wrote my first book in 2022, "No more books!" Yet here we are with another book. You are always a great supporter of my various hobbies and business ventures. I can't thank you enough for all the support you give me. I have many hopes and dreams so I know how difficult it is to put up with me. My success is only thanks to your support. What are your thoughts on book number three?

Thanks to Michael Heppell. You gave me the initial seed for this book, which started me on the path to writing again. Your superb Team 17 brought this book to life after we had the fantastic Day 17 conference in Durham City. Team 17 is something really special, and you've helped bring together an amazing group of positive and diverse people. Originally, it was your Write That Book programme that turned me into a writer. There is nothing quite like holding your own book and saying, "I'm a published author." So, thank you again for helping make a dream a reality and I can now say I'm an author with two books to my name!

Thanks to Chris Skitt for sharing the details of your solar quote with me. Writing a book involves research, and getting hold of these live documents can be difficult. However, they add substance to my writing. So thanks!

Thanks to my PA, Keely French. I know you look at my life in bemusement, wondering why I put myself under so much pressure. But I couldn't have done it without you keeping my life under control. Plus a big thanks for reading over a couple of chapters and giving me honest feedback.

Thanks to Adam Cambrook for reading my chapter on tax relief and salary sacrifice and providing invaluable feedback. That afternoon where you, Chris Race, and I discussed the order of the chapters was a time where we couldn't agree. But having people on my team with whom I can discuss things is so essential, so thanks to both of you for your thoughts.

Thanks again to Steven Holmberg, my editor, for doing such a great job with this book. Your heart must have sunk when I suggested another book but you're so good at it. How do you feel about book three?

A special mention to Jessica Jones: When you read my first book, you sent me a really long email about all the areas you'd enjoyed. Being an author is isolating and I often feel full of self-doubt. It was fantastic that you took the time to write to me, and your words in that email convinced me that another book might just work. Thank you so much!

Thanks to everyone who shared ideas for my bonus chapter on my social media. As a small token of my appreciation, I have included all your names in the book.

Thanks to all my colleagues at Orange Umbrella and Abode Living. You're a great team that supports me and works tirelessly with me. Without you all, I'd never have had the time to be an innovator and develop ideas like writing a book.

I could thank so many others, but I'll leave it there for now. I do appreciate all the people in my life who support me, and there are many of you so a heartfelt thank you even if you don't get a mention.

AUTHOR BIO

I describe myself as a family man, a triathlete, and an entrepreneur. I'm enthusiastic about life and find it hard to sit still. I've written this book to help people looking for ways to beat the cost of living crisis. I started my first business in 2003 and it has been a rollercoaster of learning from my own mistakes. When it comes to mistakes I've always turned to science in my quest for answers. It's this quest that led me to realise there are many ways we can apply science to our business problems. This led me to write my first book, The Science of Business.

My day job is running a small accountancy practice that employs nine staff members and focuses on the SME sector. The practice uses the latest technology to provide an efficient approach to managing client record keeping. I'm also the Financial Director for a local letting agency and I own a small property portfolio. I trained as a computer programmer and ran a web development agency for over ten years before starting the accountancy practice with my wife in 2012. I have been working for Northumbria University as an Associate Lecturer since 2011, teaching subjects such as Graduate Enterprise, Entrepreneurship & Creativity, E-business, Innovation, and the government-backed Help to Grow program. I have guest lectured on executive MBA programs and acted as a business mentor.

In my personal life, I'm a mad keen triathlete and love going away in my campervan. I travel across the UK in my van with my wife and two boys, taking part in triathlon races.

Printed in Great Britain
by Amazon